DRAW EDWARD!

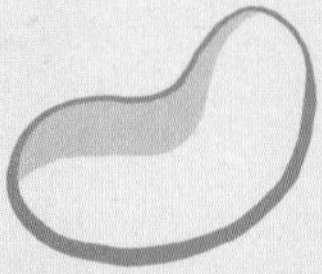

Step 1

Step 2

Step 3

Step 4

Sleeping

Walking

Trotting

Running (fast!)

Sweet dance moves

Play time

Snack time

Party time

Content

Angry

Surprised

Space explorer

Ogres Awake!

James Sturm
Andrew Arnold
Alexis Frederick-Frost

:01
First Second
New York

C'mon, Edward! Bring it back!!
LET'S GO!
CHOP CHOP!!!
RUMBLE
Oh, great. Thunder.
Weird. No rain clouds in the sky.
Edward! Fetching means bringing the stick BACK.
C'mon, let's go inside before it starts to rain. Edward?
What're you looking at, buddy?

THAT WASN'T THUNDER!
IT WAS OGRES!
GIANT OGRES!
And when they wake up, they'll attack the kingdom!

UMBLE
WHEEZE
SNORE!

Quick, Edward! We have to go warn the king!

WHEN OGRES WAKE UP, THEY **CRUSH!**
THEY **SMASH!**
THEY **DESTROY!**

THEY EAT PEOPLE! AND HORSES!!

LOWER THE GATE! LOWER THE GATE!!!
THWUMP

I'll cut through the kitchen— IT'S FASTER!
OUT OF THE WAY!
CRASH!
Sorry about that, but this is an emergency!

YOUR HIGHNESS! THE OGRES ARE HERE! THE OGRES ARE HERE!
One moment. I am reading my favorite comic.

PUT THAT COMIC AWAY! I SAW OGRES! GIANT OGRES!!! THEY'RE ASLEEP IN THE MEADOW!

WHEN THE OGRES WAKE UP, THE KINGDOM MUST BE READY!
SHARPEN OUR BLADES! ASSEMBLE THE ARMY!
PACK SOME SNACKS! PREPARE FOR BATTLE! NO SURRENDER!
HEY!!! THIS IS SERIOUS! STOP READING THAT COMIC!

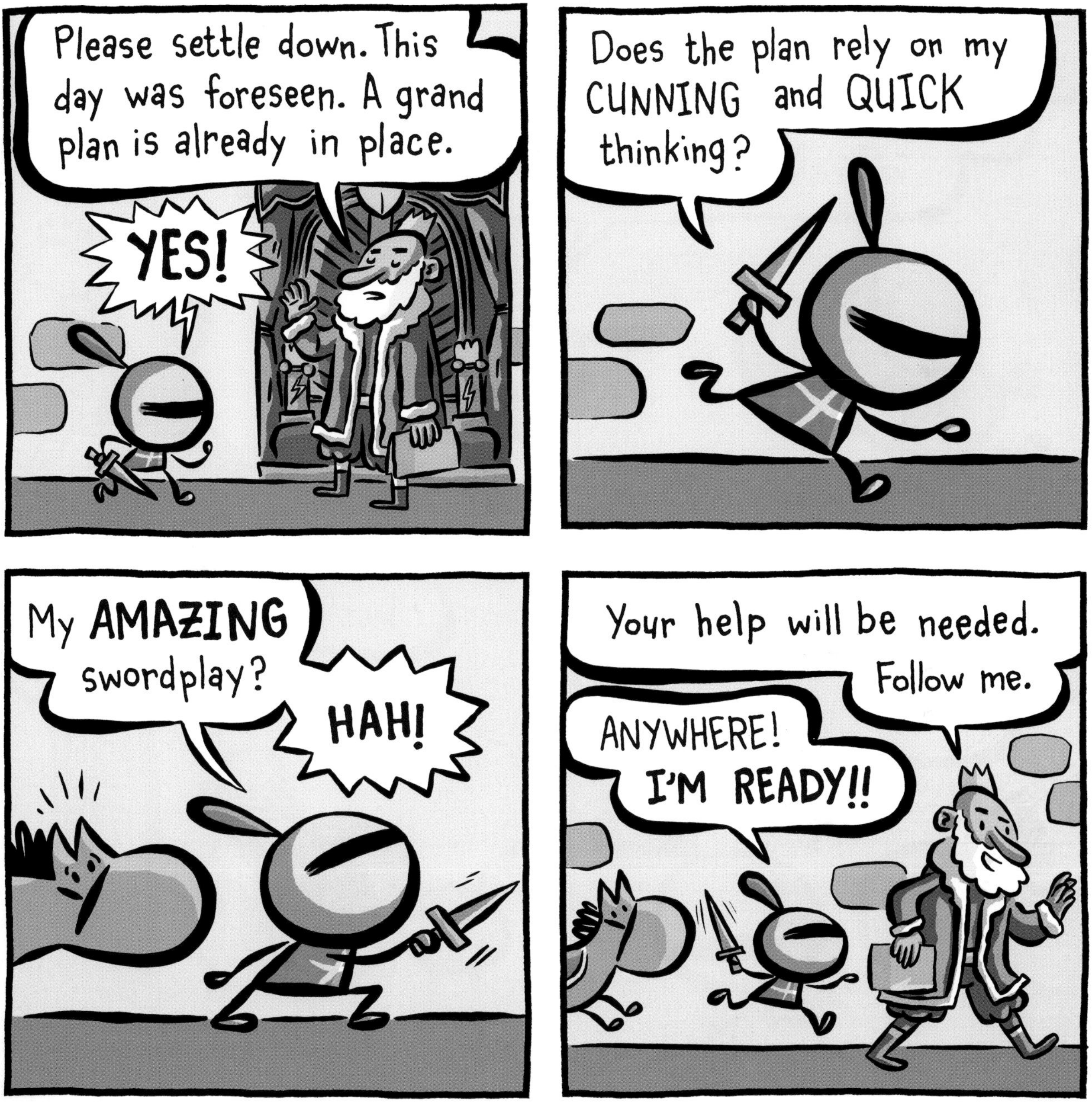
Please settle down. This day was foreseen. A grand plan is already in place.
YES!
Does the plan rely on my CUNNING and QUICK thinking?
My AMAZING swordplay?
HAH!
Your help will be needed. Follow me.
ANYWHERE! I'M READY!!

To the furious rapids of the White River! To the darkest shadows of the Black Mountains! To the Distant Shores of the Unknown!
Lead on, great ruler! Tell me where to go and I will serve with all my heart.
Just through this door will be fine.

BEHOLD...
THE GRAND PLAN!
Hello. Are you here to help? We could use it.
Huh?

I don't get it. This is just a... a... smelly ol' onion patch.
EXCUSE me...?!

It is NOT just onions!
There are beets and sweet potatoes...
And lima beans and corn and...

THIS IS MY **GARDEN!**
And these are the garden gnomes!
Howdy!
Hey! Leave the corn alone!!!
This is all wrong! We need soldiers, not garden gnomes!
We're making WAR, not a salad!

We must act NOW!
FINALLY!
We agree with the knight—we must act now.

We have readied your steed.
He is ready for action!
C'mon, Edward...

As for you, knight, are you as good with that sword as they say...?
Of course.
Then this is for you.
A vegetable peeler?
Yes, a monumental task lies ahead.
Follow me.
Your highness! How about we pour BOILING WATER on the giants?
Boiling is important...

But first you must peel potatoes and carrots.
WHOA!
This must be a test!

This is a challenge like no other!
FOR KING! FOR COUNTRY! ARRRRGGGHHHH!!!
SLICE! SLICE!
PEEL! PEEL!

I... I... did it.
PANT, PANT
Take THAT potatoes!!!
Well done, knight! But our job isn't done yet!
We have to get the potatoes to the kitchen!

QUICK, GNOMES! Into the pots! There's no time to lose!
Now I get it!

You're wizards DISGUISED as garden gnomes!
YOU'RE MAKING A MAGIC POTION! BRILLIANT!
I need parsley, STAT!
Will it turn the ogres into snails?!
No!

WILL IT PUT THE OGRES BACK TO **SLEEP?!**
WILL IT MAKE ME **300 FEET** TALL AND GIVE ME **HEAT VISION** AND **ROBOT ARMS?**
Is it done yet?!
YAWN!
IT BETTER BE!!!
The giants are waking up!

STRETCH
RUB RUB
YAWN!
GRUMBLE
MARCH!
MARCH!

ARGGHH!
ARGHHH!
POUND!
POUND!
POUND!

THEY'RE ABOUT TO BREAK THROUGH!
GRAB THE SWORDS! GRAB THE SHIELDS!
POUND! POUND!
GRAB THE BOWLS! GRAB THE SPOONS!
POUND! POUND!
POUND!

CRASH!

POSITIONS, GNOMES!
FOR KING! FOR COUNTRY!

Stand ready!
We're all going to be eaten!!!

ARRRRGH!

SNIFF
SNIFF
Hey, what's that smell?

Sweet potato stew. It's delicious.
Old family recipe. Please join us for a meal. Everything is ready.
I don't believe this.
Do ogres like hot sauce?

And thus, the kingdom was spared!
I NEVER REALIZED HOW **CRANKY** WE OGRES ARE WHEN WE FIRST WAKE UP!
LOW BLOOD SUGAR IS NO JOKE!
THAT WAS **DELICIOUS!**
So glad you enjoyed the stew!
I peeled the potatoes!

Later that day...
Boy, those ogres left quite a mess!
Clean-up is going to take FOREVER.

All in all, things worked out pretty good, I suppose.
The ogres didn't destroy the kingdom and you got a giant-sized portion of potato stew.
Still, I'm a little disappointed...
I hope in our next adventure, I'm 300 feet tall and have heat vision AND robot arms.
THE END!

First Second
New York

Published by First Second
First Second is an imprint of Roaring Brook Press, a division of
Holtzbrinck Publishing Holdings Limited Partnership
175 Fifth Avenue, New York, New York 10010

Library of Congress Control Number: 2015944388

ISBN: 978-1-59643-653-4

FIRST EDITION

First edition 2016
Printed in China by Macmillan Production (Asia) Ltd.,
Kowloon Bay, Hong Kong (Vendor Code: 10)

1 3 5 7 9 10 8 6 4 2

BY ART WE LIVE

OGRES AWAKE was drawn and colored in Adobe Photoshop using a Wacom tablet.
Text was hand-lettered on Vellum paper using Staedtler pigment liner pens.

DRAW THE GNOMES!